MŒRIS
IN THE MUSEUM OF THE LIGATURE
Œ

- Why there is not a key for the ligature œ? - *Mæris* asked.

Jorge A. Rodríguez
(JAR)

Text and Illustrations

Text and Illustrations: Jorge A. Rodríguez (JAR)
© 2015 Jorge A. Rodríguez (JAR) All rights reserved.
ISBN-13: 978-1519394330
ISBN-10: 1519394330
E-mail: jarrodriguezve@gmail.com
Facebook: Jorge A. Rodriguez Jar
Twitter: @jar_rodriguez
http://www.amazon.com/Jorge-Rodriguez/e/B00TCP6436

My best wishes *vœux*
to all of those
who from the heart *cœur*
read this work *œuvre*
and
also to those who
only give it
a glance *un coup d'œil*

JAR

Mæris, sitting down in his computer discovers how the ligature *æ* appears.

- Why there is not a key for the ligature *æ*? - He wondered…

In his keyboard, he didn't find a direct way to write the ligature *æ*, he had to pulse: "insert", "Symbol"; then, slip through the displacement bar, look for and select the ligature *æ*, in lower-case presentation or capital.

When selecting the ligature *æ*, in lower-case, he realizes that the official name of this letter appears in the inferior part of the emergent window: LATIN SMALL LIGATURE OE, code of character: 0153 of Unicode hex, keys: Alt + 0156. And this is what *Mæris* does now: looking at the keyboard maintains the key "Alt" pressed and marks the numbers 0, 1, 5, 6; and when he releases the key "Alt": the ligature *æ* appears to him, in lower-case.

Ligature œ Ligature œ Ligature œ Ligature œ
Mœris Mœris Mœris Mœris Mœris Mœris Mœris
Ligature œ Ligature œ Ligature œ Ligature œ
Mœris Mœris Mœris Mœris Mœris Mœris Mœris
Ligature œ Ligature œ Ligature œ Ligature œ
Mœris Mœris Mœris Mœris Mœris Mœris Mœris
Ligature œ Ligature œ Ligature œ Ligature œ
Mœris Mœris Mœris Mœris Mœris Mœris Mœris
Ligature œ L   e Ligature œ
Mœris Mœris   Mœris Mœris
Ligature œ L   e Ligature œ
Mœris Mœris   Mœris Mœris
Ligature œ L   e Ligature œ
Mœris Mœris   ŒE   Mœris Mœris
Ligature œ L   e Ligature œ
Mœris Mœris   Mœris Mœris
Ligature œ L   e Ligature œ
Mœris Mœris   Mœris Mœris
Ligature œ L   e Ligature œ
Mœris Mœris   Mœris Mœris
Ligature œ L   e Ligature œ
Mœris Mœris Mœris Mœris Mœris Mœris Mœris
Ligature œ Ligature œ Ligature œ Ligature œ
Mœris Mœris Mœris Mœris Mœris Mœris Mœris
Ligature œ Ligature œ Ligature œ Ligature œ
Mœris Mœris Mœris Mœris Mœris Mœris Mœris
Ligature œ Ligature œ Ligature œ Ligature œ
Mœris Mœris Mœris Mœris Mœris Mœris Mœris
Ligature œ Ligature œ Ligature œ Ligature œ
Mœris Mœris Mœris Mœris Mœris Mœris Mœris
Ligature œ Ligature œ Ligature œ Ligature œ

- Wow, how complicated… why there is not a key for the ligature *œ*, and done? … - *Mœris* wondered.

Then, he selected the ligature in capital and the name appeared: CAPITAL LATIN LIGATURE OE, Code of character: 0152, of Unicode hex, Keys: Alt + 0140. Equally, when maintaining pressed the key "Alt" and writing that number, the ligature *œ* appeared, this time in capital. Also, he realized that those keys could be programmed and this way, place the ligature *œ* with another combination of keys…

- Well, that complicates even more the things, because other computers can have other keys assigned … but to select: "insert" and subsequently "symbol" to slip through the displacement bar, look for and select the ligature *œ* pulse "insert" at the end, is more secure…and there it will appear… Why There is simply not a key for this letter?... - *Mœris* wondered again.

Musée de la Ligature œ Musée de la Ligature œ
Mœris Mœris Mœris Mœris Mœris Mœris Mœris
Musée de la Ligature œ Musée de la Ligature œ
Mœris Mœris Mœris Mœris Mœris Mœris Mœris
Musée de la Ligature œ Musée de la Ligature œ
Mœris Mœris Mœris Mœris Mœris Mœris Mœris
Musée de la Ligature œ Musée de la Ligature œ
Mœris Mœris Mœris Mœris Mœris Mœris Mœris
Musée de la L   la Ligature œ
Mœris Mœris   Mœris Mœris
Musée de la L   la Ligature œ
Mœris Mœris   Mœris Mœris
Musée de la L   la Ligature œ
Mœris Mœris   ŒE   Mœris Mœris
Musée de la L   la Ligature œ
Mœris Mœris   Mœris Mœris
Musée de la L   la Ligature œ
Mœris Mœris   Mœris Mœris
Musée de la L   la Ligature œ
Mœris Mœris Mœris Mœris Mœris Mœris Mœris
Musée de la Ligature œ Musée de la Ligature œ
Mœris Mœris Mœris Mœris Mœris Mœris Mœris
Musée de la Ligature œ Musée de la Ligature œ
Mœris Mœris Mœris Mœris Mœris Mœris Mœris
Musée de la Ligature œ Musée de la Ligature œ
Mœris Mœris Mœris Mœris Mœris Mœris Mœris
Musée de la Ligature œ Musée de la Ligature œ
Mœris Mœris Mœris Mœris Mœris Mœris Mœris
Musée de la Ligature œ Musée de la Ligature œ

Mæris' Father calls him: - Listen to this - *Mæris'* Father says, while he continues reading a newspaper -: … The Plastic Artist donates his artworks *œuvres d´art* for the collection of the Museum of the Ligature Œ […] Museum in which are all those words written with the ligature *œ* […]

- Is there a Museum of the Ligature Œ?! - *Mæris* asked surprised…

- Yes, continue reading and look where it is. This way you will be able to go to visit it and continue with your collection of words in your notebook - the father said.

- Look, dad! … It is also near, I will visit it tomorrow - *Mæris* said.

Mæris, always had his notebook at hand, ready to go writing down those things that interested him… This notebook was something very special which he took everywhere, very different with his notebooks of the school.

Œuvre d'art Œuvre d'art Œuvre d'art Œuvre d'art
Musée de la Ligature œ Musée de la Ligature œ
Œuvre d'art Œuvre d'art Œuvre d'art Œuvre d'art
Musée de la Ligature œ Musée de la Ligature œ
Œuvre d'art Œuvre d'art Œuvre d'art Œuvre d'art
Musée de la Ligature œ Musée de la Ligature œ
Œuvre d'art Œuvre d'art Œuvre d'art Œuvre d'art
Musée de la Ligature œ Musée de la Ligature œ
Œuvre d'art Œuvre d'art Œuvre d'art Œuvre d'art
Musée de la I   la Ligature œ
Œuvre d'art Œuvre d'art Œuvre d'art Œuvre d'art
Musée de la I   la Ligature œ
Œuvre d'art Œuvre d'art Œuvre d'art Œuvre d'art
Musée de la I   la Ligature œ
Œuvre d'art Œuvre d'art Œuvre d'art Œuvre d'art
Musée de la I   ŒŒ   la Ligature œ
Œuvre d'art Œuvre d'art Œuvre d'art Œuvre d'art
Musée de la I   la Ligature œ
Œuvre d'art Œuvre d'art Œuvre d'art Œuvre d'art
Musée de la I   la Ligature œ
Œuvre d'art Œuvre d'art Œuvre d'art Œuvre d'art
Musée de la I   la Ligature œ
Œuvre d'art Œuvre d'art Œuvre d'art Œuvre d'art
Musée de la Ligature œ Musée de la Ligature œ
Œuvre d'art Œuvre d'art Œuvre d'art Œuvre d'art
Musée de la Ligature œ Musée de la Ligature œ
Œuvre d'art Œuvre d'art Œuvre d'art Œuvre d'art
Musée de la Ligature œ Musée de la Ligature œ
Œuvre d'art Œuvre d'art Œuvre d'art Œuvre d'art
Musée de la Ligature œ Musée de la Ligature œ
Œuvre d'art Œuvre d'art Œuvre d'art Œuvre d'art
Musée de la Ligature œ Musée de la Ligature œ
Œuvre d'art Œuvre d'art Œuvre d'art Œuvre d'art

Mæris, already very early in the morning was in the Museum of the Ligature Œ… amid what seems to be a small entrance reception, with a garden, where there was a big black dog that frightened him for moments; but soon he saw that it was very friendly. To the back it could be listened the sound of a classic melody, and voices of a representation of tragic opera… *Mæris* continued walking until arriving to an entrance control where the watchman of the museum was…

- Welcome to the Museum of the Ligature Œ, you should be older than nine years old and know how to read very well, also have the available time to see all the museum rooms… go ahead - the watchman of the museum told *Mæris*.

- Very well! Thank you Mister - *Mæris* responded, a little confused by the solitary atmosphere of the museum in that moment.

Ligature œ Ligature œ Ligature œ Ligature œ
Musée de la Ligature œ Musée de la Ligature œ
Ligature œ Ligature œ Ligature œ Ligature œ
Musée de la Ligature œ Musée de la Ligature œ
Ligature œ Ligature œ Ligature œ Ligature œ
Musée de la Ligature œ Musée de la Ligature œ
Ligature œ Ligature œ Ligature œ Ligature œ
Musée de la Ligature œ Musée de la Ligature œ
Ligature œ Ligature œ Ligature œ Ligature œ
Musée de la Ligature œ Musée de la Ligature œ
Ligature œ Ligature œ Ligature œ Ligature œ
Musée de la Ligature œ Musée de la Ligature œ
Ligature œ Ligature œ Ligature œ Ligature œ

MŒRIS

Musée de la Ligature œ Musée de la Ligature œ
Ligature œ Ligature œ Ligature œ Ligature œ
Musée de la Ligature œ Musée de la Ligature œ
Ligature œ Ligature œ Ligature œ Ligature œ
Musée de la Ligature œ Musée de la Ligature œ
Ligature œ Ligature œ Ligature œ Ligature œ
Musée de la Ligature œ Musée de la Ligature œ
Ligature œ Ligature œ Ligature œ Ligature œ
Musée de la Ligature œ Musée de la Ligature œ
Ligature œ Ligature œ Ligature œ Ligature œ
Musée de la Ligature œ Musée de la Ligature œ
Ligature œ Ligature œ Ligature œ Ligature œ
Musée de la Ligature œ Musée de la Ligature œ
Ligature œ Ligature œ Ligature œ Ligature œ

Some more steps and he arrived to a museum room of grammatical information and historical investigation of the ligature *æ*. Many books press articles and magazines… as well as, a computer that was of exclusive use of investigation, just as it highlighted it the small sign that was glued to the monitor. However, *Mœris* came a little closer and saw that in that keyboard there was not any key to write, of first intention, the ligature *æ*.

Grammatical information and verbs were the name of that first museum room… There the verbs written with the ligature *æ* were. Framed each one and exposed in the wall, showing the way how they were conjugated in their different verbal tenses. The same as the prefix: *Œn* (o) of the Greek oinos: wine.

Musée de la Ligature œ Musée de la Ligature œ
maniobrar *manœuvrer*, asquear *écœurer*, esquejar
œilletonner, obrar *œuvrer*, maniobrar *manœuvrer*,
asquear *écœurer*, esquejar *œilletonner*, obrar *œuvrer*
maniobrar *manœuvrer*, asquear *écœurer*, esquejar
Musée de la Ligature œ Musée de la Ligature œ
œilletonner, obrar *œuvrer*, maniobrar *manœuvrer*,
asquear *écœurer*, esquejar *œilletonner*, obrar *œuvrer*
Musée de la Ligature œ Musée de la Ligature œ
maniobrar *manœuvrer*, asquear *écœurer*, esquejar
Musée de la Ligature œ Musée de la Ligature œ
œilletonner, obrar *œuvrer*, maniobrar *manœuvrer*,

MŒRIS

asquear *écœurer*, esquejar *œilletonner*, obrar *œuvrer*
Musée de la Ligature œ Musée de la Ligature œ
maniobrar *manœuvrer*, asquear *écœurer*, esquejar
Musée de la Ligature œ Musée de la Ligature œ
œilletonner, obrar *œuvrer*, maniobrar *manœuvrer*,
Musée de la Ligature œ Musée de la Ligature œ
asquear *écœurer*, esquejar *œilletonner*, obrar *œuvrer*
Musée de la Ligature œ Musée de la Ligature œ
maniobrar *manœuvrer*, asquear *écœurer*, esquejar
Musée de la Ligature œ Musée de la Ligature œ
œilletonner, obrar *œuvrer*, maniobrar *manœuvrer*,
Musée de la Ligature œ Musée de la Ligature œ
asquear *écœurer*, esquejar *œilletonner*, obrar *œuvrer*
Musée de la Ligature œ Musée de la Ligature œ

- To maneuver *manœuvrer*, to disgust *écœurer*, to cut *œilletonner*, to work *œuvrer*… - *Mæris* read.

- To cut? *œilletonner*? - *Mæris* wondered -, "to sow cuts" *œilletons* - said in the information explaining the meaning of the verb.

And continued reading and seeing the illustrations of what meant "to sow cuts" *œilletons* and its procedure… *Mæris* took out his notebook and wrote down this new word…

- What are you doing, boy? - The watchman of the museum asked *Mæris*.

- Writing down the words written with the ligature *œ* - *Mæris* said.

- Very well; but in all the museum rooms you will find, at the end of the walk, a list with all the words that are written with the ligature *œ* of that room. And at the end of the museum, you will be able to take the complete listing… acquire some articles and books, if you want - the watchman explained to him.

Musée de la Ligature œ Musée de la Ligature œ
meilleurs vœux meilleurs vœux meilleurs vœux
Musée de la Ligature œ Musée de la Ligature œ
meilleurs vœux meilleurs vœux meilleurs vœux
Musée de la Ligature œ Musée de la Ligature œ
meilleurs vœux meilleurs vœux meilleurs vœux

Meillerus Vœux

BONNE
ANNÉE

- What museum room comes now, Mr.? - *Mœris* asked.

- Continue ahead and you will find some very curious things, you can pass to the museum room of the objects. - The watchman of the museum told him.

When entering to the museum room of the objects, the first thing that finds *Mœris* is a cabinet with many stamps or bells *vœux* and greeting cards *cartes de vœux* of all type: "My best wishes" *Meilleurs vœux*, you could read it in several cards… with many hearts *cœurs*, of all the forms and sizes. Beside the cabinet, a lit chimney, in the bottom of the chimney a big sign that indicated: "fireback" *contrecœur. Mœris* realized that the fireback *contrecœur* or fire wall, is the attaché or the support of the chimney that protects the wall of the far end.

Musée de la Ligature œ Musée de la Ligature œ
œillets, œilletons œillets œilletons œillets œilletons
Musée de la Ligature œ Musée de la Ligature œ
œillets, œilletons œillets œilletons œillets œilletons
Musée de la Ligature œ Musée de la Ligature œ
œillets, œilletons œillets œilletons œillets œilletons
Musée de la Ligature œ Musée de la Ligature œ
œillets, œilletons œillets œilletons œillets œilletons
Musée de la Ligature œ Musée de la Ligature œ
œillets, œilletons œillets œilletons œillets œilletons
Musée de la Ligature œ Musée de la Ligature œ
œillets, œilletons œillets œilletons œillets œilletons
Musée de la Ligature œ Musée de la Ligature œ
œillets, œilletons œillets œilletons œillets œilletons
Musée de la Ligature œ Musée de la Ligature œ
œillets, œilletons œillets œilletons œillets œilletons
Musée de la Ligature œ Musée de la Ligature œ
œillets, œilletons œillets œilletons œillets œilletons
Musée de la Ligature œ Musée de la Ligature œ
œillets, œilletons œillets œilletons œillets œilletons
Musée de la Ligature œ Musée de la Ligature œ
œillets, œilletons œillets œilletons œillets œilletons
Musée de la Ligature œ Musée de la Ligature œ
œillets, œilletons œillets œilletons œillets œilletons
Musée de la Ligature œ Musée de la Ligature œ
œillets, œilletons œillets œilletons œillets œilletons
Musée de la Ligature œ Musée de la Ligature œ

Mæris continued seeing objects: a hairdryer *fœhn* (French of Switzerland), a book of samples of different types of knots *nœuds*, buttonholes of clothes *œils*, eyelets *œillets* in shoes and wallets, viewer of doors *œilletons*, peepholes or viewers *œilletons* of some weapons and several adapting eyeglasses for photographic cameras that create the eye *œil* fish Effect of Poisson.

Also, a great circular stone of a mill in which was pointed out in its center, the heart *cœur* of the mill: the *œillard*.

The following objects *Mæris* already knew them, they were the *œillères* in all its presentations: glass washes eyes *œillères*, eye patch of pirates *œillères* (*cache-œil*) and eye *œil* cover of the horses *œillères*, these last ones were on a horse head, real size, very impressive.

Musée de la Ligature œ Musée de la Ligature œ
Musée de la Ligature œ Musée de la Ligature œ
Musée de la Ligature œ Musée de la Ligature œ
Musée de la Ligature œ Musée de la Ligature œ
Musée de la Ligature œ Musée de la Ligature œ
Musée de la Ligature œ Musée de la Ligature œ
Musée de la Ligature œ Musée de la Ligature œ
Musée de la Ligature œ Musée de la Ligature œ
Musée de la Ligature œ Musée de la Ligature œ
Musée de la Ligature œ Musée de la Ligature œ
Musée de la Ligature œ Musée de la Ligature œ
Musée de la Ligature œ Musée de la Ligature œ
Musée de la Ligature œ Musée de la Ligature œ
Musée de la Ligature œ Musée de la Ligature œ
Musée de la Ligature œ Musée de la Ligature œ
Musée de la Ligature œ Musée de la Ligature œ

œil de bœuf

Also, he recognized an apparatus that his father had in the store of wines *œnothèque*, an oenometer *œnomètre*. To the side he saw a strange object, rectangular, with the *œrsted* name; it was a compass that had the name of a Danish scientist: *Hans Christian Œrsted*. Compass that had a metal magnetized called *œrstite*: *Œrstite*: steel, alloy of metal mixture of titanium and cobalt. Magnetic. *Œrsted*: *Unit of measure of magnetic field [...]* - one could read in the information of the compass. Already at the end of the museum room of the objects there were several of them that shared the same name: eyes of ox *œil-de-bœuf* , the viewer eyes of ox *œil-de-bœuf* were shown for the doors; different types of windows, some big ones oval and other small and circular. For the ships: skylights *œil-de-bœuf* and a compass with a small increase lens. The picture of a candy that is also called eye of ox *œil-de-bœuf*, also, some stones and seeds with the same name: eye of ox *œil-de-bœuf*.

Musée de la Ligature œ Musée de la Ligature œ
sœurette bonne-sœur belle-sœur consœur sœurette
Musée de la Ligature œ Musée de la Ligature œ
sœurette bonne-sœur belle-sœur consœur sœurette
Musée de la Ligature   e de la Ligature œ
sœurette bonne-sœur belle-sœur consœur sœurette
Musée de la Lig   la Ligature œ
sœurette bonne-sœur belle-sœur consœur sœurette
Musée de la L   Ligature œ
sœurette bonne-sœur belle-sœur consœur sœurette
Musée de la   Ligature œ
sœurette bonne-sœur belle-sœur consœur sœurette
Musée de la   Ligature œ
sœurette bonne-sœur belle-sœur consœur sœurette
Musée de la   Ligature œ
sœurette bonne-sœur belle-sœur consœur sœurette
Musée de la   Ligature œ
sœurette bonne-sœur belle-sœur consœur sœurette
Musée de la   Ligature œ
sœurette bonne-sœur belle-sœur consœur sœurette
Musée de la   Ligature œ
sœurette bonne-sœur belle-sœur consœur sœurette
Musée de la L   a Ligature œ
sœurette bonne-sœur belle-sœur consœur sœurette
Musée de la Liga   e la Ligature œ
sœurette bonne-sœur belle-sœur consœur sœurette
Musée de la Ligature   e de la Ligature œ
sœurette bonne-sœur belle-sœur consœur sœurette
Musée de la Ligature œ Musée de la Ligature œ
sœurette bonne-sœur belle-sœur consœur sœurette
Musée de la Ligature œ Musée de la Ligature œ

A picture of some clouds, indicating a small formation in the sky that one can see before a storm, equally well-known also as: eye of ox *œil-de-bœuf*. And many watches.

At the end something more: a formation of rocks, indicating the limits of the city: *pomœrium*, the Roman limits. Also some curious apparatuses called look-eggs *mire-œufs* that serve to find the transparency of the eggs *œufs* and to see the development of the fetuses *fœtus*. These apparatuses also, they could be used placing some eggs *œufs* and looking through them…

- How good and interesting! … And I am only by the second museum room; my dad will love this place… I will soon tell him to come! - *Mœris* thought.

Mœris leaves the museum room of the objects. From a distance he sees some mannequins dressed in a different way, to natural size… it is the section of: family and professions to which he comes closer…

Musée de la Ligature œ Musée de la Ligature œ
Stœchiometrie Stœchiometrie Stœchiometrie
Musée de la Liga de la Ligature œ
Stœchiometrie Stœchiometrie Stœchiometrie
Musée de la Liga de la Ligature œ
Stœchiometrie Stœchiometrie Stœchiometrie
Musée de la Liga de la Ligature œ
Stœchiometrie Stœchiometrie Stœchiometrie
Musée de la Liga de la Ligature œ
Stœchiometrie Stœchiometrie Stœchiometrie
Musée de la Liga de la Ligature œ
Stœchiometrie Stœchiometrie Stœchiometrie
Musée de la Liga de la Ligature œ
Stœchiometrie Stœchiometrie Stœchiometrie
Musée de la Liga de la Ligature œ
Stœchiometrie Stœchiometrie Stœchiometrie
Musée de la Liga de la Ligature œ
Stœchiometrie Stœchiometrie Stœchiometrie
Musée de la Liga de la Ligature œ
Stœchiometrie Stœchiometrie Stœchiometrie
Musée de la Liga de la Ligature œ
Stœchiometrie Stœchiometrie Stœchiometrie
Musée de la Liga de la Ligature œ
Stœchiometrie Stœchiometrie Stœchiometrie
Musée de la Liga de la Ligature œ
Stœchiometrie Stœchiometrie Stœchiometrie
Musée de la Liga de la Ligature œ
Stœchiometrie Stœchiometrie Stœchiometrie
Musée de la Ligature œ Musée de la Ligature œ

- I cannot believe it! ... It is my family! … My dad, that of the glass of wine, is the enologist *œnologue*; my little sister, *sœurette*; my aunt; the nun bonne-*sœur* that comes to be the sister-in-law *belle-sœur* of my father and even my mother this way to indicate the relationship with my aunt, her sister *sœur*… My friend, the acolyte! *enfant de chœur!* ; that lady that works with my father; his partner *consœur* and even my uncle that before worked as journeyman *manœuvre* and that is now unoccupied *désœuvré*. They are all with their respective attires and the names that identify their professions. A doctor specialized in Stoichiometry *Stœchiometrie* is at the end… - *Mœris* thought very astonished. This was incredible… the resemblance was enormous, or perhaps, it was only the fatigue of *Mœris*… Already confused, he decided to go home and he would continue another day the journey of the museum. He would continue in the following museum room; that of the animals…

Musée de la Ligature œ Musée de la Ligature œ
pique-bœuf œil de bœuf héron garde-bœuf
Musée de la Ligature œ Musée de la Ligature œ
pique-bœuf œil de bœuf héron garde-bœuf
Musée de la Ligature œ Musée de la Ligature œ
pique-bœuf œil de bœuf héron garde-bœuf
Musée de la Ligature œ Musée de la Ligature œ
pique-bœuf œil de bœuf héron garde-bœuf
Musée de la Ligature œ Musée de la Ligature œ
pique-bœuf œil de bœuf héron garde-bœuf
Musée de la Ligature œ Musée de la Ligature œ

BŒUF

pique-bœuf œil de bœuf héron garde-bœuf
Musée de la Ligature œ Musée de la Ligature œ
pique-bœuf œil de bœuf héron garde-bœuf
Musée de la Ligature œ Musée de la Ligature œ
pique-bœuf œil de bœuf héron garde-bœuf
Musée de la Ligature œ Musée de la Ligature œ
pique-bœuf œil de bœuf héron garde-bœuf
Musée de la Ligature œ Musée de la Ligature œ
pique-bœuf œil de bœuf héron garde-bœuf
Musée de la Ligature œ Musée de la Ligature œ
pique-bœuf œil de bœuf héron garde-bœuf
Musée de la Ligature œ Musée de la Ligature œ
pique-bœuf œil de bœuf héron garde-bœuf
Musée de la Ligature œ Musée de la Ligature œ

The next day, in the museum, *Mœris* enters to the museum room of the animals. All represented natural size, even, some were dissected. He thought that he wouldn't find many animals, but he was mistaken, this museum room was one of the most numerous and amazing…

An enormous Ox *Bœuf* that was with all its work tools to plow the earth, with its great name written in the inferior part, with its respective information… on it a small bird: a *chop-bœuf* and to the side a *herón garde-bœuf*, white bird of long neck.

  - Wow, how impressive! … - *Mœris* said.

Continuing a head was the oldest ancestor in the elephants the *Mœritherium*, another strange animal that *Mœris* had never seen. Later he saw some beautiful blue birds called *calœnas*.

Musée de la Ligature œ Musée de la Ligature œ
Cœlacanthe Cœlacanthe Cœlacanthe Cœlacanthe
Musée de la Ligature œ Musée de la Ligature œ
Cœlacanthe Cœlacanthe Cœlacanthe Cœlacanthe
Musée de la Ligature œ Musée de la Ligature œ
Cœlacanthe Cœlacanthe Cœlacanthe Cœlacanthe
Musée de la Ligature œ Musée de la Ligature œ
Cœlacanthe Cœlacanthe Cœlacanthe Cœlacanthe
Musée de la Ligature œ Musée de la Ligature œ
Cœlacanthe Cœlacanthe Cœlacanthe Cœlacanthe
Muse de la Ligat lg Cœlacanthe Cœlacanthe
Musée Cœlacanthe Cœlacanthe Cœlacanthe Cœlacanthe
Musée de la Lig Cœlacanthe Cœlacanthe Cœlacanthe
Musée de la Ligature œ Musée de la Ligature œ
Cœlacanthe Cœlacanthe Cœlacanthe Cœlacanthe
Musée de la Ligature œ Musée de la Ligature œ
Cœlacanthe Cœlacanthe Cœlacanthe Cœlacanthe
Musée de la Ligature œ Musée de la Ligature œ
Cœlacanthe Cœlacanthe Cœlacanthe Cœlacanthe
Musée de la Ligature œ Musée de la Ligature œ
Cœlacanthe Cœlacanthe Cœlacanthe Cœlacanthe
Musée de la Ligature œ Musée de la Ligature œ
Cœlacanthe Cœlacanthe Cœlacanthe Cœlacanthe
Musée de la Ligature œ Musée de la Ligature œ

In a huge fishbowl... an enormous fish name Coelacanth *Cœlacanthe* explained in the records of information that it was a reproduction, because these fish had already extinguished a long time ago, although in fact, they have recently found some examples in the depths of the sea... In some small screens a video was presented, where some investigators filmed a Coelacanth *Cœlacanthe* live in the deepest in the sea of Indonesia. Also in the same fishbowl, to the other end, there was kind of a jellyfish of name *cœlentéré* of clear colors... The *œuvée* that is a female fish transporting its eggs *œufs*, was also there. Continuing the journey there was a snake *cœlopeltis*. A little later on... - Oh, how disgusting! *écœurement* - *Mœris* exclaimed.

Musée de la Ligature œ Musée de la Ligature œ
œdicnemes œdicnemes œdicnemes œdicnemes
Musée de la Ligature œ Musée de la Ligature œ
œdicnemes œdicnemes œdicnemes œdicnemes
Musée de la Ligature œ Musée de la Ligature œ
œdicnemes œdicnemes œdicnemes œdicnemes
Musée de la Ligature œ Musée de la Ligature œ
œdicne mes œdicnemes œdicnemes
Musée de la Ligature œ Musée de la Ligature œ
œdicn mes œdicnemes œdicnemes
Musée de la Ligature œ Musée de la Ligature œ
œdicnemes œdi emes œdicnemes mes
Musée de la Ligature œ Musée de la Ligature œ
œdicnemes œdicnemes œdicnemes mes
Musée de la Ligature œ Musée de la Ligature œ
œdicnemes œdicnemes œdicne dicnemes
Musée de la Ligature œ Musée de la Ligature œ
œdicnemes œdicnemes œdicne s dicnemes
Musée de la Ligature œ Musée de la Ligature œ
œdicnemes œdicn mes dicnem œdicnemes
Musée de la Ligature œ Musée de la Ligature œ
œdicnemes œdicne es dicner œdicnemes
Musée de la Ligature œ Musée de la Ligature œ
œdicnemes œdicnes dicner œdicnemes
Musée de la Ligature œ Musée de la Ligature œ
œdicnemes œdicnemes œdicnemes œdicnemes
Musée de la Ligature œ Musée de la Ligature œ

In some jars flies and larvas of name *cœnomyie* (coenomyia ferruginea) and another: *œstre*. The larvas: *œstridé* and the *œstrus ovis*. Others of name: *cœnures* larvas of Taenia (Tænia) that produces in the animals an illness called cenurosis. Without a doubt this was the most disgusting *écœurer*. Later on, in another jar there was a beautiful butterfly *Dianthœcia* and another smaller of name *Mœlibée*. Also several gray birds of big yellow eyes, long paws with three fingers name: *œdicnèmes*. To the side one smaller, an *œnanthe*. And another denominated *pœcile*. These were presented in their nests, to remember that also the word eggs *œufs*, was written with the ligature *œ*. A great image of a red bird was exposed, identified as: The *phœnix*, mythical bird endowed with longevity and characterized by its capacity to reborn after having been consumed under the effect of its own fire. It symbolizes the cycles of death and resurrection.

Musée de la Ligature œ Musée de la Ligature œ
cercopithèque de l'hœst cercopithèque de l'hœst
Musée de la Ligature œ Musée de la Ligature œ
cercopithèque de l'hœst cercopithèque de l'hœst
Musée de la Ligature œ Musée de la Ligature œ
cercopithèque de l'hœst cercopithèque de l'hœst
Musée de la Ligature œ Musée de la Ligature œ
cercopithèque de l'hœst cercopithèque de l'hœst
Musée de la Ligature œ Musée de la Ligature œ
cercopithèque de l'hœst cercopithèque de l'hœst
Musée de la Ligature œ Musée de la Ligature œ
cercopithèque de l'hœst cercopithèque de l'hœst
Musée de la Ligature œ Musée de la Ligature œ
cercopithèque de l'hœst cercopithèque de l'hœst
Musée de la Ligature œ Musée de la Ligature œ
cercopithèque de l'hœst cercopithèque de l'hœst
Musée de la Ligature œ Musée de la Ligature œ
cercopithèque de l'hœst cercopithèque de l'hœst
Musée de la Ligature œ Musée de la Ligature œ
cercopithèque de l'hœst cercopithèque de l'hœst
Musée de la Ligature œ Musée de la Ligature œ
cercopithèque de l'hœst cercopithèque de l'hœst
Musée de la Ligature œ Musée de la Ligature œ

At the end of the museum room of the animals some graphics that showed their reproductive cycle, with some more words: *œstral, œstrale, œstraux* and *œstrus*. In a great cage leaving to the garden, it was a seated monkey on some branches: the *l'hœst cercopithèque* (*Cercopithecus lhœsti*) almost the whole thing of black hair, with its white neck and red eyes. This surprised *Mœris* a lot, because it was one of the few alive animals that was in the museum…

The nature, that was the group of words that were in the garden… at the beginning of the journey pictures with the word heart *cœur*: heart of lettuce *cœur de laitue*, cabbage, melon, etc. In an external cabinet the seeds called eyes of ox *œil-de-bœuf* were exhibited, some big flowers very yellow, equally called eyes of ox *œil-de-bœuf*, well-known in some countries as arnica. And a great display of fruits: soursop (Annona reticulata), apples, cherries, cabbage and tomatoes; known as "ox heart" *cœur de bœuf*.

Musée de la Ligature œ Musée de la Ligature œ
cœur de bœuf cœur de bœuf cœur de bœuf
Musée de la Ligature œ Musée de la Ligature œ
cœur de bœuf cœur de bœuf cœur de bœuf
Musée de la Ligature œ Musée de la Ligature œ
cœur de bœuf cœur de bœuf cœur de bœuf
Musée de la Ligature œ Musée de la Ligature œ
cœur de bœuf cœur de bœuf cœur de bœuf
Musée de la Ligature œ Musée de la Ligature œ
cœur de bœuf cœur de bœuf cœur de bœuf
Musée de la Ligature œ Musée de la Ligature œ
cœur de bœuf BŒUF cœur de bœuf
Musée de la Ligature œ Musée de la Ligature œ
cœur de bœuf cœur de bœuf cœur de bœuf
Musée de la Ligature œ Musée de la Ligature œ
cœur de bœuf cœur de bœuf cœur de bœuf
Musée de la Ligature œ Musée de la Ligature œ
cœur de bœuf cœur de bœuf cœur de bœuf
Musée de la Ligature œ Musée de la Ligature œ
cœur de bœuf cœur de bœuf cœur de bœuf
Musée de la Ligature œ Musée de la Ligature œ
cœur de bœuf cœur de bœuf cœur de bœuf
Musée de la Ligature œ Musée de la Ligature œ
cœur de bœuf cœur de bœuf cœur de bœuf
Musée de la Ligature œ Musée de la Ligature œ

- I remember these flowers… they are the same ones that I saw once in the works *œuvres* of the exhibition of that foreign artist… that exhibited the names of the flowers with the pictures… and these seeds are in the same types of jars that he used in his artworks *œuvres d´art - Mæris* thought.

Sowed in the garden there were the flowers of eyes of ox *œil-de-bœuf* and, the most impressive thing: many carnations *œillets* of several colors. The aroma was unmistakable: carnations *œillets* everywhere with their sprouts *œilletons*.

Mæris, continues the journey.

- And now… what is this?... - he wondered.

It was a small lagoon with form of heart *cœur*… *Mæris* doesn't find, at the moment any explanatory sign; but he walks a little more and he reads an information: *œnanthe*: plant herbaceous aquatic, hairless and poisonous […].

Musée de la Ligature œ Musée de la Ligature œ
œillets œillets œillets œnanthe œillets œillets œillets
Musée de la Ligature œ Musée de la Ligature œ
œillets œillets œillets œnanthe œillets œillets œillets
Musée de la Ligature œ Musée de la Ligature œ
œillets œillets œillets œnanthe œillets œillets œillets
Musée de la Ligature œ Musée de la Ligature œ
œillets œillets œillets œnanthe œillets œillets œillets
Musée de la Ligature œ Musée de la Ligature œ
œillets œillets œillets œnanthe œillets œillets œillets
Musée de la Ligature œ Musée de la Ligature œ
œillets œillets œillets œnanthe œillets œillets œillets
Musée de la Ligature œ Musée de la Ligature œ
œillets œillets œillets œnanthe œillets œillets œillets
Musée de la Ligature œ Musée de la Ligature œ
œillets œillets œillets œnanthe œillets œillets œillets
Musée de la Ligature œ Musée de la Ligature œ
œillets œillets œillets œnanthe œillets œillets œillets
Musée de la Ligature œ Musée de la Ligature œ
œillets œillets œillets œnanthe œillets œillets œillets
Musée de la Ligature œ Musée de la Ligature œ
œillets œillets œillets œnanthe œillets œillets œillets
Musée de la Ligature œ Musée de la Ligature œ
œillets œillets œillets œnanthe œillets œillets œillets
Musée de la Ligature œ Musée de la Ligature œ
œillets œillets œillets œnanthe œillets œillets œillets
Musée de la Ligature œ Musée de la Ligature œ

Mœris continues walking through the garden… meeting some plants with flowers color fuchsia identified as of the family of the oenothera *œnothera* ou *œnothère*. Other flowers even redder and more beautiful: the *gœthée*. They could also be observed great quantity of big and small palms, of those common palms that there are everywhere, identified as: *phœnix*, of several types.

The garden finished, but still the section of the nature continued … In a cabinet, the pictures of a plant called: Poppy *œillette*, well-known equally as poppy; seeds and jars of oil that is extracted from it; the oil of poppy *huile d'œillette*, in its two versions: eatable and for artistic use. *Mœris* continued reading the information of this plant, it explained that they exhibited the pictures that there was not the plant, because it was illegal, since from it a drug was extracted: the heroine.

Musée de la Ligature œ Musée de la Ligature œ
lœss lœss lœss lœss lœss lœss lœss lœss lœss
Musée de la Ligature œ Musée de la Ligature œ
lœss lœss lœss lœss lœss lœss lœss lœss lœss
Musée de la Ligature œ Musée de la Ligature œ
lœss lœss lœss lœss lœss lœss lœss lœss lœss
Musée de la Ligature œ Musée de la Ligature œ
lœss lœss lœss lœss lœss lœss lœss lœss lœss
Musée de la Ligature œ Musée de la Ligature œ
lœss lœss lœss lœss lœss lœss lœss lœss lœss
Musée de la Ligature œ Musée de la Ligature œ
lœss lœss lœss lœss lœss lœss lœss lœss lœss
Musée de la Ligature œ Musée de la Ligature œ
lœss lœss lœss lœss lœss lœss lœss lœss lœss
Musée de la Ligature œ Musée de la Ligature œ
lœss lœss lœss lœss lœss lœss lœss lœss lœss
Musée de la Ligature œ Musée de la Ligature œ
lœss lœss lœss lœss lœss lœss lœss lœss lœss
Musée de la Ligature œ Musée de la Ligature œ
lœss lœss lœss lœss lœss lœss lœss lœss lœss
Musée de la Ligature œ Musée de la Ligature œ
lœss lœss lœss lœss lœss lœss lœss lœss lœss
Musée de la Ligature œ Musée de la Ligature œ
lœss lœss lœss lœss lœss lœss lœss lœss lœss
Musée de la Ligature œ Musée de la Ligature œ
lœss lœss lœss lœss lœss lœss lœss lœss lœss
Musée de la Ligature œ Musée de la Ligature œ
lœss lœss lœss lœss lœss lœss lœss lœss lœss
Musée de la Ligature œ Musée de la Ligature œ

He sees the garden again and now he notices an earth heap in the distance that he over saw. He comes closer… and sees that the earth heap also shows a new word: *læss*. Reads the information attentively and continues the journey.

- Wow, the things that are written with the ligature *œ*, are everywhere… - *Mœris* thought.

Mœris again enters to the area of the nature and now he notices some enormous pictures… A great landscape with clouds and explanatory graphics of what is the *fœhn* effect of: a warm and a dry wind that is, in occasions, in the top of the mountains; it is surprisingly also a synonym of the hairdryers *fœhn* (French of Switzerland)… Another picture showed the outer space, with many stars that pointed out the nebula call: eye of cat *œil de chat*. And there *Mœris* found his sister's *sœurette* name that referred to an asteroid: *Clœlia*: asteroid number 661, discovered by Metcalf in February of the year 1908.

Musée de la Ligature œ Musée de la Ligature œ
Clœlia Clœlia Clœlia Clœlia Clœlia Clœlia Clœlia
Musée de la Ligature œ Musée de la Ligature œ
Clœlia Clœlia Clœlia Clœlia Clœlia Clœlia Clœlia
Musée de la Ligature œ Musée de la Ligature œ
Clœlia Clœlia Clœlia Clœlia Clœlia Clœlia Clœlia
Musée de la Ligature œ Musée de la Ligature œ
Clœlia Clœlia Clœlia Clœlia Clœlia Clœlia Clœlia
Musée de la Ligature œ Musée de la Ligature œ
Clœlia Clœlia Clœlia Clœlia Clœlia Clœlia Clœlia
Musée de la Ligature œ Musée de la Ligature œ
Clœlia Clœlia Clœlia Clœlia Clœlia Clœlia Clœlia
Musée de la Ligature œ Musée de la Ligature œ
Clœlia Clœlia Clœlia Clœlia Clœlia Clœlia Clœlia
Musée de la Ligature œ Musée de la Ligature œ
Clœlia Clœlia Clœlia Clœlia Clœlia Clœlia Clœlia
Musée de la Ligature œ Musée de la Ligature œ
Clœlia Clœlia Clœlia Clœlia Clœlia Clœlia Clœlia
Musée de la Ligature œ Musée de la Ligature œ
Clœlia Clœlia Clœlia Clœlia Clœlia Clœlia Clœlia
Musée de la Ligature œ Musée de la Ligature œ
Clœlia Clœlia Clœlia Clœlia Clœlia Clœlia Clœlia
Musée de la Ligature œ Musée de la Ligature œ
Clœlia Clœlia Clœlia Clœlia Clœlia Clœlia Clœlia
Musée de la Ligature œ Musée de la Ligature œ
Clœlia Clœlia Clœlia Clœlia Clœlia Clœlia Clœlia
Musée de la Ligature œ Musée de la Ligature œ

To *Mœris* it is still necessary for him to go through more museum rooms; but he should leave… and he will return another day.

- Did you pick up the lists of words at the end of each museum room? - the watchman of the museum asked *Mœris*.

- Yes, here I take them; I will come later with my father to finish the journey, Mister. - *Mœris* said.

Before leaving the museum *Mœris* has another concern…

- Every time the back music is listened more and more… is it in all the museum rooms, does it have something to do with the ligature *œ*?... - *Mœris* asked the watchman.

- When you return again and finish the journey, you will find the answer - the watchman told him.

Mœris arrives at his house…

Musée de la Ligature œ Musée de la Ligature œ
fœtus fœtaux fœtus fœtaux fœtus fœtaux fœtus
Musée de la Ligature œ Musée de la Ligature œ
fœtus fœtaux fœtus fœtaux fœtus fœtaux fœtus
Musée de la Ligature œ Musée de la Ligature œ
fœtus fœtaux fœtus fœtaux fœtus fœtaux fœtus
Musée de la Ligature œ Musée de la Ligature œ
fœtus fœtaux fœtus fœtaux fœtus fœtaux fœtus
Musée de la Ligature œ Musée de la Ligature œ
fœtus fœtaux fœtus fœtaux fœtus fœtaux fœtus
Musée de la Ligature œ Musée de la Ligature œ
fœtus fœtaux fœtus fœtaux fœtus fœtaux fœtus
Musée de la Ligature œ Musée de la Ligature œ
fœtus fœtaux fœtus fœtaux fœtus fœtaux fœtus
Musée de la Ligature œ Musée de la Ligature œ
fœtus fœtaux fœtus fœtaux fœtus fœtaux fœtus
Musée de la Ligature œ Musée de la Ligature œ
fœtus fœtaux fœtus fœtaux fœtus fœtaux fœtus
Musée de la Ligature œ Musée de la Ligature œ
fœtus fœtaux fœtus fœtaux fœtus fœtaux fœtus
Musée de la Ligature œ Musée de la Ligature œ
fœtus fœtaux fœtus fœtaux fœtus fœtaux fœtus
Musée de la Ligature œ Musée de la Ligature œ
fœtus fœtaux fœtus fœtaux fœtus fœtaux fœtus
Musée de la Ligature œ Musée de la Ligature œ

- Did you already finish gathering words in the museum, *Mæris*? - The father asked.

- In fact, no but… could you come with me when I go again?... - *Mæris* asked.

- Of course, tomorrow in the morning we can go! - the father answered him, foreseeing that he wanted to continue the journey as soon as possible…

The following day, very early day in the morning, *Mæris* and his father were already at the doors of the Museum of the Ligature Œ. There he saw again the great black dog in the entrance, but this time he saw on its house a sign: Belgian shepherd: *Grænendael*, he realized that it was another alive animal that presented the museum…

Musée de la Ligature œ Musée de la Ligature œ.
asa-fœtida asa-fœtida asa-fœtida asa-fœtida asa-fœtida
Musée de la Ligature œ Musée de la Ligature œ.
asa-fœtida asa-fœtida asa-fœtida asa-fœtida asa-fœtida
Musée de la Ligature œ Musée de la Ligature œ.
asa-fœtida asa-fœtida asa-fœtida asa-fœtida asa-fœtida
Musée de la Ligature œ Musée de la Ligature œ.
asa-fœtida asa-fœtida asa-fœtida asa-fœtida asa-fœtida
Musée de la Ligature œ Musée de la Ligature œ.
asa-fœtida asa-fœtida asa-fœtida asa-fœtida asa-fœtida
Musée de la Ligature œ Musée de la Ligature œ.
asa-fœtida asa-fœtida asa-fœtida asa-fœtida asa-fœtida
Musée de la Ligature œ Musée de la Ligature œ.
asa-fœtida asa-fœtida asa-fœtida asa-fœtida asa-fœtida
Musée de la Ligature œ Musée de la Ligature œ.
asa-fœtida asa-fœtida asa-fœtida asa-fœtida asa-fœtida
Musée de la Ligature œ Musée de la Ligature œ.
asa-fœtida asa-fœtida asa-fœtida asa-fœtida asa-fœtida
Musée de la Ligature œ Musée de la Ligature œ.
asa-fœtida asa-fœtida asa-fœtida asa-fœtida asa-fœtida
Musée de la Ligature œ Musée de la Ligature œ.
asa-fœtida asa-fœtida asa-fœtida asa-fœtida asa-fœtida
Musée de la Ligature œ Musée de la Ligature œ.
asa-fœtida asa-fœtida asa-fœtida asa-fœtida asa-fœtida
Musée de la Ligature œ Musée de la Ligature œ.
asa-fœtida asa-fœtida asa-fœtida asa-fœtida asa-fœtida
Musée de la Ligature œ Musée de la Ligature œ.
asa-fœtida asa-fœtida asa-fœtida asa-fœtida asa-fœtida
Musée de la Ligature œ Musée de la Ligature œ

Already when entering *Mœris* showed his father the last section in the museum room of the nature to see his sister's *sœurette* name *Clœlia* and later, they entered the room of the body and the emotions. In this; it was coelom *cœlome*, the first word that was presented, graphically its location was indicated in the small earth worms; and other bigger graphics indicated their presence in the human body. This last graphic indicated the location of the eye *œil*, the heart *cœur*, esophagus *œsophage* and the first part of the thick intestine the cecum *cœcum*.

Subsequently something very particular and impressive: in some jars, closed tightly, several fetuses *fœtus* and images of fetal positions *fœtaux* could be seen.

Musée de la Ligature œ Musée de la Ligature œ
cœnesthésie cœnesthésie cœnesthésie cœnesthésie
Musée de la Ligature œ Musée de la Ligature œ
cœnesthésie cœnesthésie cœnesthésie cœnesthésie
Musée de la Ligature œ Musée de la Ligature œ
cœnesthésie cœnesthésie cœnesthésie cœnesthésie
Musée de la Ligature œ Musée de la Ligature œ
cœnesthésie cœnesthésie cœnesthésie cœnesthésie
Musée de la Ligature œ Musée de la Ligature œ
cœnesthésie cœnesthésie cœnesthésie cœnesthésie
Musée de la Ligature œ Musée de la Ligature œ
cœnesthésie cœnesthésie cœnesthésie cœnesthésie
Musée de la Ligature œ Musée de la Ligature œ
cœnesthésie cœnesthésie cœnesthésie cœnesthésie
Musée de la Ligature œ Musée de la Ligature œ
cœnesthésie cœnesthésie cœnesthésie cœnesthésie
Musée de la Ligature œ Musée de la Ligature œ
cœnesthésie cœnesthésie cœnesthésie cœnesthésie
Musée de la Ligature œ Musée de la Ligature œ
cœnesthésie cœnesthésie cœnesthésie cœnesthésie
Musée de la Ligature œ Musée de la Ligature œ
cœnesthésie cœnesthésie cœnesthésie cœnesthésie
Musée de la Ligature œ Musée de la Ligature œ
cœnesthésie cœnesthésie cœnesthésie cœnesthésie
Musée de la Ligature œ Musée de la Ligature œ
cœnesthésie cœnesthésie cœnesthésie cœnesthésie
Musée de la Ligature œ Musée de la Ligature œ

An apparatus to examine the esophagus *œsophage*: the esophagoscopy *œsophagoscope*; and an optic tube that is introduced inside the body: the coelioscopy *cœlioscopie*, showing several images taken with this apparatus. They showed a lot of information of surgical interventions, using this apparatus in diverse cases. Images of the body could be observed showing ocular, brain, lung and of skin edemas *œdèmes*, but *Mœris* and his father didn't want to see them …leaving from there. *Mœris*, saw from a distance a small jar with movable lid, in which one could smell a sample of asafetida *fœtida*. When coming closer…

- Uuff! How disgusting *écœurement* - *Mœris* said, retiring from there, because the bad scent caused him nauseas and a slight spasm *haut-he-cœur* in the stomach…

-

Musée de la Ligature œ Musée de la Ligature œ
Mu œ
Mu de la Ligature œ Musée de la Liga œ
Mu de la Ligature œ Musée de la Liga œ
Mu de la Ligature œ Musée de la Liga œ
Mus de la Ligature œ Musée de la Liga œ
Mu de la Ligature œ Musée de la Liga œ
M de la Ligature ŒE Musée de la Liga œ
Mu de la Ligature œ Musée de la Liga œ
Mu de la Ligature œ Musée de la Liga œ
Mu de la Ligature œ Musée de la Liga œ
Mu de la Ligature œ Musée de la Liga œ
Mu de la Ligature œ Musée de la Liga œ
Mus de la Ligature œ Musée de la Liga œ
Musée de la Ligature Musée de la Ligature œ
Musée de la Ligature œ Musée de la Ligature œ

Asafetida *fœtida*, unpleasant sensation that affects the esophagus *œsophage*. And like it says here…- continued reading *Mœris'* father - it forces the sick person to constantly swallow saliva.

- Look, dad!… - *Mœris* said, remembering the name of the illness that his mother had suffered. Celiac *Cœliaque*, was read next, with its corresponding information and some considerations for its treatment. Subsequently, x-rays were shown in that a well-known intestinal obstruction was pointed out as: Cecum volvulus *volvulus du cœcum*; and the ileocecal region *iléo-cœcale*.

At the end of this museum room of the body the presence of alcohol was shown in the blood, due to the intake of wine in excess: *œnilisme*. And a big apparatus of x- rays, and many x-rays of the body that reminded the discoverer of the x- rays: *Wilhelm Conrad Rœntgen*.—

Musée de la Ligature œ Musée de la Ligature œ
œnologie: œn(o), œnantique, œnilisme, œnotheque
Musée de la Ligature œ Musée de la Ligature œ
œnologie: œn(o), œnantique, œnilisme, œnotheque
Musée de la Ligature œ Musée de la Ligature œ
œnologie: œn(o), œnantique, œnilisme, œnotheque
Musée de la Ligature œ Musée de la Ligature œ
œnologie: œn(o), œnantique, œnilisme, œnotheque
Musée de la Ligature œ Musée de la Ligature œ
œnologie: œn(o), œnantique, œnilisme, œnotheque
Musée de la Ligature œ Musée de la Ligature œ
œnologie: œn(o), œnantique, œnilisme, œnotheque
Musée de la Ligature œ Musée de la Ligature œ
œnologie: œn(o), œnantique, œnilisme, œnotheque
Musée de la Ligature œ Musée de la Ligature œ
œnologie: œn(o), œnantique, œnilisme, œnotheque
Musée de la Ligature œ Musée de la Ligature œ
œnologie: œn(o), œnantique, œnilisme, œnotheque
Musée de la Ligature œ Musée de la Ligature œ
œnologie: œn(o), œnantique, œnilisme, œnotheque
Musée de la Ligature œ Musée de la Ligature œ
œnologie: œn(o), œnantique, œnilisme, œnotheque
Musée de la Ligature œ Musée de la Ligature œ
œnologie: œn(o), œnantique, œnilisme, œnotheque
Musée de la Ligature œ Musée de la Ligature œ
œnologie: œn(o), œnantique, œnilisme, œnotheque
Musée de la Ligature œ Musée de la Ligature œ

Leaving the museum room of the body and the emotions, there was the word: coenesthesia *cœnesthésie*: vague and widespread sensation that one has of the own internal organism. To culminate they presented some illustrations in humorous style, hearts *cœurs*, expressing: emotion, love, passion. Other hearts *cœurs* were related with the word: disgust *écœurer*, to which corresponded several situations and emotions. Another heart *cœur* represented the bitterness *rancœur*, showing us feelings and displeasure expressions, of acting scoldingly, unwillingly á *contrecœur*.

The museum room of the knowledge and the awareness continued next, it was divided in sections by areas of knowledge.

Musée de la Ligature œ Musée de la Ligature œ
Œdipe Roi, Thouthmosis III (Mœris), Œdipe Roi
Musée de la Ligature œ Musée de la Ligature œ
Œdipe Roi, Thouthmosis III (Mœris), Œdipe Roi
Musée de la Ligature œ Musée de la Ligature œ
Œdipe Roi, Thouthmosis III (Mœris), Œdipe Roi
Musée de la Ligature œ Musée de la Ligature œ
Œdipe Roi, Thouthmosis III (Mœris), Œdipe Roi
Musée de la Ligature œ Musée de la Ligature œ
Œdipe Roi, Thouthmosis III (Mœris), Œdipe Roi
Musée de la Ligature œ Musée de la Ligature œ
Œdipe Roi, Thouthmosis III (Mœris), Œdipe Roi
Musée de la Ligature œ Musée de la Ligature œ
Œdipe Roi, Thouthmosis III (Mœris), Œdipe Roi
Musée de la Ligature œ Musée de la Ligature œ
Œdipe Roi, Thouthmosis III (Mœris), Œdipe Roi
Musée de la Ligature œ Musée de la Ligature œ
Œdipe Roi, Thouthmosis III (Mœris), Œdipe Roi
Musée de la Ligature œ Musée de la Ligature œ
Œdipe Roi, Thouthmosis III (Mœris), Œdipe Roi
Musée de la Ligature œ Musée de la Ligature œ
Œdipe Roi, Thouthmosis III (Mœris), Œdipe Roi
Musée de la Ligature œ Musée de la Ligature œ

This way in the area that corresponded to Art there were the words: work *œuvre*; artwork *œuvre d'art* masterpiece *chef d'œuvre*; musical works, humorous and amusing: *hors d'œuvre*; trap to the eye *trompe-l'œil*: deceiving effect; and a case of oil painting with oil of poppy *huile d'œillete*.

In the area of the religion stood out the words: nun *bonne-sœur*, choir *chœur*, acolyte *enfant de chœur*, sacred heart *sacre cœur* and the explanation with respect to the ecumenical *œcumenique*.

In the scientific section there was a small laboratory, where the estrogens *œstrogènes* were shown, the coenzyme *cœnzyme*, was presented the chemical connections characteristic of the stoichiometry *stœchiométrie*, and the unit of atomic measure the angstrom, *angstrœm*. It was also there the *homœopathie* word introduced by Samuel Hahnemann.

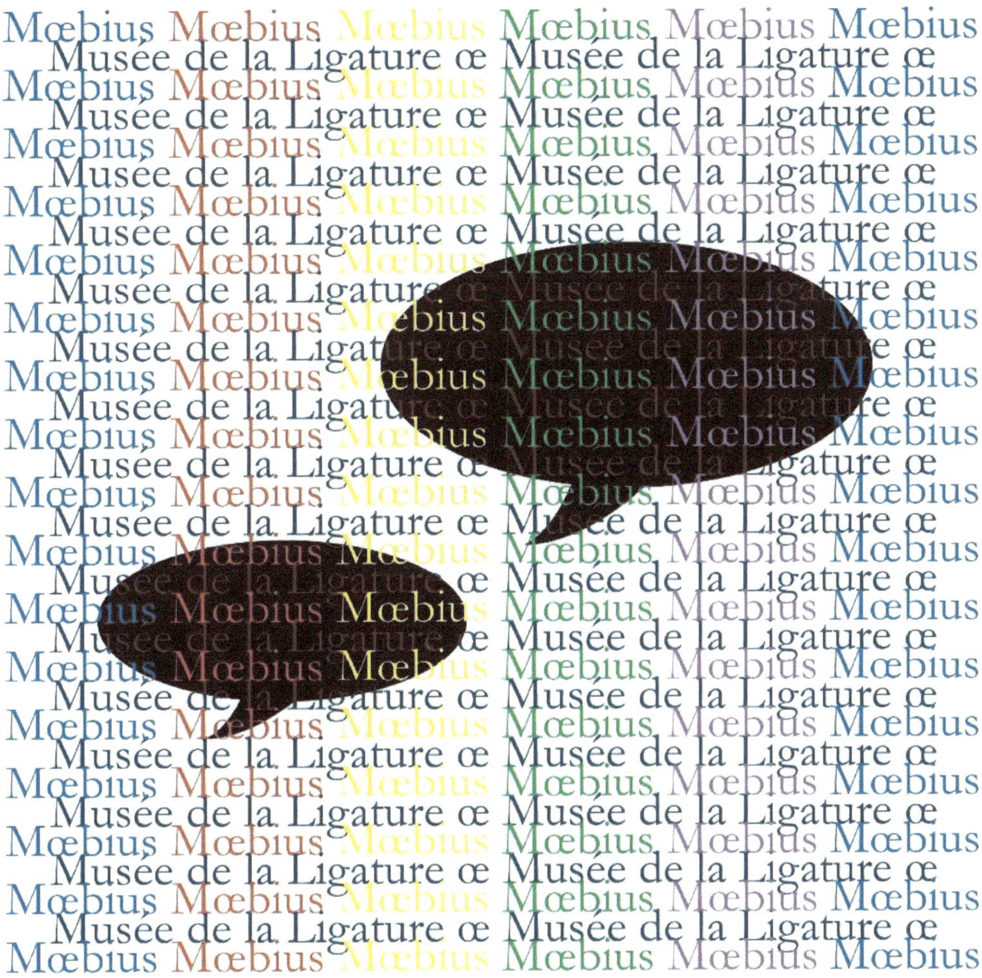
Mœbius Mœbius Mœbius Mœbius Mœbius Mœbius
Musée de la Ligature œ Musée de la Ligature œ
Mœbius Mœbius Mœbius Mœbius Mœbius Mœbius
Musée de la Ligature œ Musée de la Ligature œ
Mœbius Mœbius Mœbius Mœbius Mœbius Mœbius
Musée de la Ligature œ Musée de la Ligature œ
Mœbius Mœbius Mœbius Mœbius Mœbius Mœbius
Musée de la Ligature œ Musée de la Ligature œ
Mœbius Mœbius Mœbius Mœbius Mœbius Mœbius
Musée de la Ligature œ Musée de la Ligature œ
Mœbius Mœbius Mœbius Mœbius Mœbius Mœbius
Musée de la Ligature œ Musée de la Ligature œ
Mœbius Mœbius Mœbius Mœbius Mœbius Mœbius
Musée de la Ligature œ Musée de la Ligature œ
Mœbius Mœbius Mœbius Mœbius Mœbius Mœbius
Musée de la Ligature œ Musée de la Ligature œ
Mœbius Mœbius Mœbius Mœbius Mœbius Mœbius
Musée de la Ligature œ Musée de la Ligature œ
Mœbius Mœbius Mœbius Mœbius Mœbius Mœbius
Musée de la Ligature œ Musée de la Ligature œ
Mœbius Mœbius Mœbius Mœbius Mœbius Mœbius
Musée de la Ligature œ Musée de la Ligature œ
Mœbius Mœbius Mœbius Mœbius Mœbius Mœbius
Musée de la Ligature œ Musée de la Ligature œ
Mœbius Mœbius Mœbius Mœbius Mœbius Mœbius
Musée de la Ligature œ Musée de la Ligature œ
Mœbius Mœbius Mœbius Mœbius Mœbius Mœbius
Musée de la Ligature œ Musée de la Ligature œ
Mœbius Mœbius Mœbius Mœbius Mœbius Mœbius
Musée de la Ligature œ Musée de la Ligature œ
Mœbius Mœbius Mœbius Mœbius Mœbius Mœbius
Musée de la Ligature œ Musée de la Ligature œ
Mœbius Mœbius Mœbius Mœbius Mœbius Mœbius

In sociology, the terms were explained: ecumene *œkoumène* that designates the inhabited lands and synoecism *synœcisme*: that means regrouping of towns or cities under one same administration…

- Look, dad is the oenology! *œnologie* - *Mœris* exclaimed while he looked to everywhere…
Big barrels of wine, bottles, glasses of several types, pictures of big cellars, books and enologists' *œnólogues* pictures, testing wine, measure apparatuses and relating words to the enology *œnologie*: *œn* (o), *œnantique*, *œnilisme*, *œnotheque*. Recipients of several materials and colors of names: enócoe *œnochoé*. *Mœris´* father explained to him the use of those objects… And to conclude this museum room, the kitchen section had numerous *rœsti* recipes: Potato omelette traditional Swiss cuisine.

JAR JAR JAR JAR JAR JAR JAR JAR JAR JAR
Musée de la Ligature œ Musée de la Ligature œ
JAR JAR JAR JAR JAR JAR JAR JAR JAR JAR
Musée de la Ligature œ Musée de la Ligature œ
JAR JAR JAR JAR JAR JAR JAR JAR JAR JAR
Musée de la Ligature œ Musée de la Ligature œ
JAR JAR JAR JAR JAR JAR JAR JAR JAR JAR
Musée de la Ligature œ Musée de la Ligature œ
JAR JAR JAR JAR JAR JAR JAR JAR JAR JAR
Musée de la Ligature œ Musée de la Ligature
JAR JAR JAR JAR JAR JAR JAR JAR JAR JAR
Musée de la Ligature œ Musée de la Ligature œ
JAR JAR JAR JAR JAR JAR JAR JAR JAR JAR
Musée de la Ligature œ Musée de la Ligature œ
JAR JAR JAR JAR JAR JAR JAR JAR JAR JAR
Œ Musée de la Ligature œ Musée de la
JAR JAR JAR JAR JAR JAR JAR JAR JAR JAR
Musée de la Ligature œ Musée de la Ligature œ
JAR JAR JAR JAR JAR JAR JAR JAR JAR JAR
Musée de la Ligature œ Musée de la Ligature œ
JAR JAR JAR JAR JAR JAR JAR JAR JAR JAR
Musée de la Ligature œ Musée de la Ligature œ
JAR JAR JAR JAR JAR JAR JAR JAR JAR JAR
Musée de la Ligature œ Musée de la Ligature œ
JAR JAR JAR JAR JAR JAR JAR JAR JAR JAR
Musée de la Ligature œ Musée de la Ligature œ
JAR JAR JAR JAR JAR JAR JAR JAR JAR JAR
Musée de la Ligature œ Musée de la Ligature œ
JAR JAR JAR JAR JAR JAR JAR JAR JAR JAR

Famous characters, it was one of the last museum room of the journey, it began with one of the kings from the old Egypt; the king Thouthmosis III (*Mœris*). In whose honor the lake was baptized *Mœris*...

Having passed from the enology *œnologie* to the famous characters and meeting with the King *Mœris*, was an experience, in which father and son could be identified, putting on evidence the great affection that had *Mœris* for his father... it was as if those museum rooms were there only for them.

Other characters could be observed in this museum room with a lot of information of Oedipus King *Œdipe Roi*; the Greek tragedy could be read and watched in a small video. *Clœlia*, the Roman virgin, her history could be read in this section and *Mœris* remembered his little sister *sœurette*.

JAR Mœris JAR Mœris JAR Mœris JAR Mœris JAR
Musée de la Ligature œ Musée de la Ligature œ
JAR Mœris JAR Mœris JAR Mœris JAR Mœris JAR
Musée de la Ligature œ Musée de la Ligature œ
JAR Mœris JAR Mœris JAR Mœris JAR Mœris JAR
Musée de la Ligature œ Musée de la Ligature œ
JAR Mœris JAR Mœris JAR Mœris JAR Mœris JAR
Musée de la Ligature œ Musée de la Ligature œ
JAR Mœris JAR Mœris JAR Mœris JAR Mœris JAR
Musée de la Ligature œ Musée de la Ligature œ
JAR Mœris JAR Mœris JAR Mœris JAR Mœris JAR
Musée de la Ligature œ Musée de la Ligature œ
JAR Mœris JAR Mœris JAR Mœris JAR Mœris JAR
Musée de la Ligature œ Musée de la Ligature œ
JAR Mœris JAR Mœris JAR Mœris JAR Mœris JAR
Musée de la Ligature œ Musée de la Ligature œ
JAR Mœris JAR Mœris JAR Mœris JAR Mœris JAR
Musée de la Ligature œ Musée de la Ligature œ
JAR Mœris JAR Mœris JAR Mœris JAR Mœris JAR
Musée de la Ligature œ Musée de la Ligature œ
JAR Mœris JAR Mœris JAR Mœris JAR Mœris JAR
Musée de la Ligature œ Musée de la Ligature œ
JAR Mœris JAR Mœris JAR Mœris JAR Mœris JAR
Musée de la Ligature œ Musée de la Ligature œ
JAR Mœris JAR Mœris JAR Mœris JAR Mœris JAR
Musée de la Ligature œ Musée de la Ligature œ
JAR Mœris JAR Mœris JAR Mœris JAR Mœris JAR
Musée de la Ligature œ Musée de la Ligature œ
JAR Mœris JAR Mœris JAR Mœris JAR Mœris JAR
Musée de la Ligature œ Musée de la Ligature œ
JAR Mœris JAR Mœris JAR Mœris JAR Mœris JAR

Many other famous characters filled the museum room: a French General; *Marie Pierre Kœnig*. Scientists as: *Wilhelm Conrad Rœntgen* the inventor of the x- rays; *Hans Christian Œrsted* who investigated the effects of the electromagnetism and *Emmy Nœther*, eminent mathematician, among others. Philosophers and intellectuals as: *Paul Ricœur*, of whom a great variety of books was exhibited. Many illustrations and comics of *Mœbius*. Musicians like: *Charles Kœchlin*, a great composer of classic music whose music sounded as atmosphere in the museum…

- Dad, this is the music that I told you that is always in the museum… - *Mœris* said to his father, already finishing the journey…

- Look!, *Mœris*… that is the Artist that has donated some artworks *œuvres d'art* to the museum - the father warns him.

Musée de la Ligature œ Musée de la Ligature œ
Cœlacanthe Cœlacanthe Cœlacanthe Cœlacanthe
Musée de la Ligature œ Musée de la Ligature œ
Cœlacanthe Cœlacanthe Cœlacanthe Cœlacanthe
Musée de la Ligature œ Musée de la Ligature œ
Cœlacanthe Cœlacanthe Cœlacanthe Cœlacanthe
Musée de la Ligature œ Musée de la Ligature œ
Cœlacanthe Cœlacanthe Cœlacanthe Cœlacanthe
Musée de la Ligature œ Musée de la Ligature œ
Cœlac anthe Cœlacanthe
Musée de la Ligature œ
Cœlaca nthe
Musée ture œ
Cœlaca anthe
Musée de la Liga ature œ
Cœlacanthe Cœlac Cœlacanthe
Musée de la Ligature œ Musée de la Ligature œ
Cœlacanthe Cœlacanthe Cœlacanthe Cœlacanthe
Musée de la Ligature œ Musée de la Ligature œ
Cœlacanthe Cœlacanthe Cœlacanthe Cœlacanthe
Musée de la Ligature œ Musée de la Ligature œ
Cœlacanthe Cœlacanthe Cœlacanthe Cœlacanthe
Musée de la Ligature œ Musée de la Ligature œ
Cœlacanthe Cœlacanthe Cœlacanthe Cœlacanthe
Musée de la Ligature œ Musée de la Ligature œ
Cœlacanthe Cœlacanthe Cœlacanthe Cœlacanthe
Musée de la Ligature œ Musée de la Ligature œ

The Artist that signs his artworks *œuvres d'art* like: JAR is in the Museum of the Ligature Œ, donating some artworks *œuvres d'art* , and converses with *Mæris*…

-…You will see, I have created the Illustrated Dictionary of the Ligature Œ with great effort and a lot of people's help. Also, The Museum of the ligature *œ* is my great project. It is an obligation, the ligature *œ*, it is more than a theme for me, it is my motivation to create and as a part of my investigation I should gather information, all this is necessary for the creation of my work *œuvre*… - the Artist told *Mæris*.
Mæris asks the Artist…

- How did it occur to make a museum for these words that take the ligature *œ*?, Why a museum? - He asked.

- First I will ask you something… why were you interested in these words?

ruban de mœbius ruban de mœbius ruban de mœbius
Musée de la Ligature œ Musée de la Ligature œ
ruban de mœbius ruban de mœbius ruban de mœbius
Musée de la Ligature œ Musée de la Ligature œ
ruban de mœbius ruban de mœbius ruban de mœbius
Musée de la Ligature œ Musée de la Ligature œ
ruban de mœbius ruban de mœbius ruban de mœbius
Musée de la Ligature œ Musée de la Ligature œ
ruban de mœbius ruban de mœbius ruban de mœbius
Musée de la Ligature œ Musée de la Ligature œ
ruban de mœbius ruban de mœbius ruban de mœbius
Musée de la Ligature œ Musée de la Ligature œ
ruban de mœbius ruban de mœbius ruban de mœbius
Musée de la Ligature œ Musée de la Ligature œ
ruban de mœbius ruban de mœbius ruban de mœbius
Musée de la Ligature œ Musée de la Ligature œ
ruban de mœbius ruban de mœbius ruban de mœbius
Musée de la Ligature œ Musée de la Ligature œ
ruban de mœbius ruban de mœbius ruban de mœbius
Musée de la Ligature œ Musée de la Ligature œ
ruban de mœbius ruban de mœbius ruban de mœbius
Musée de la Ligature œ Musée de la Ligature œ
ruban de mœbius ruban de mœbius ruban de mœbius
Musée de la Ligature œ Musée de la Ligature œ
ruban de mœbius ruban de mœbius ruban de mœbius
Musée de la Ligature œ Musée de la Ligature œ
ruban de mœbius ruban de mœbius ruban de mœbius
Musée de la Ligature œ Musée de la Ligature œ
ruban de mœbius ruban de mœbius ruban de mœbius
Musée de la Ligature œ Musée de la Ligature œ
ruban de mœbius ruban de mœbius ruban de mœbius

- I always had the doubt of why my name had that letter: *Mœris*..., many times I wrote it with the "o" and the "e" separate... - he explained.

- Very well... and now... How will you write your name? ... - the Artist asked.

- Well... now I believe that I will be much more pending of that, to write my name with the ligature *œ* - *Mœris* answered.

- Good, very good! That is the reason for which this museum was made - the Artist said.

- I don't understand... - *Mœris* said, something confused.

- The main reason for which this museum was created is so that who visits it uses these words, and be attentive of placing the ligature *œ*, in the words that require it; the more they are used, more time they will remain and they will exist in the conscience of each one, they won't only be museum pieces... - the Artist said.

- Yes, I understand …but… and what do we do with the words that are no longer used? Names, of animals that already extinguished like the fish for example. - *Mœris* asked.

- The coelacanth? *Cœlacanthe*? - the Artist asked.

- Yes, that one… and other animals, or plants that no longer exist - *Mœris* replied, interested.

- In that case, it is there when the museum is good to maintain alive those words, to sow conscience, to make the call for the care and the conservation. In my case as a Plastic Artist, I include those words with the ligature æ in my artworks *œuvres d'art*… to remember them, besides, all this is good, to maintain alive the ligature æ… to continue using it…, also, the ligature *æ*, is for me a metaphor of the reduction of the space… do you see how they seem to be disputing the space that they occupy, the "o" and the "e"? - the artist answered, pointing out one of his works *œuvres* -. The title of this work *œuvre* is: "*The ribbon of Mœbius*", this curious ribbon is very well-known, as a symbol in the industry of the recycling and it also represents the infinitive…-and continued the Artist conversing with *Mœris*…

Mœris would continue talking with the Artist in the Museum of the Ligature Œ and, visiting the museum rooms, inclusive, consulting in Internet the museum rooms of the virtual museum. *Mœris* became a defender of the use and the presence of the ligature œ to maintain it alive among us… Now he is always attentive, he writes and he reminds to all that:

- *Mœris*, is written with the ligature œ, please…

The End.

Text and Illustrations: Jorge A. Rodríguez (JAR)
© 2015 Jorge A. Rodríguez (JAR) All rights reserved.
ISBN-13: 978-1519394330
ISBN-10: 1519394330
E-mail: jarrodriguezve@gmail.com
Facebook: Jorge A. Rodriguez Jar
Twitter: @jar_rodriguez
http://www.amazon.com/Jorge-Rodriguez/e/B00TCP6436

OTHER WORKS PUBLISHED

MŒRIS And the Illustrated Dictionary of the Ligature Œ